A Journey to the Light

Putting It All Out in the Open…

Brennan R. Wegener

2022

Trilogy Christian Publishers
A Wholly Owned Subsidiary of Trinity Broadcasting Network
2442 Michelle Drive
Tustin, CA 92780

10 9 8 7 6 5 4 3 2 1
Library of Congress Cataloging-in-Publication Data is available.
ISBN 978-1-68556-224-3
ISBN 978-1-68556-225-0 (ebook)

DEDICATION

I would like to dedicate this book to my family and my two boys. I love you. Also, I dedicate this book to my veteran brothers and sisters and those currently serving in the United States Armed Services.

I dedicate this to all my Iraq and Afghanistan veterans and other veterans from any war. The struggles we face are no joke. We receive little help to deal with the transition, PTSD, traumatic brain injuries, and paranoia.

I dedicate this to the recovery community struggling with addictions and the families also struggling with the codependency and aftermath of these sad strongholds.

Ultimately this is dedicated to my God and Jesus Christ for His relentless love and for the way He allows me to live and help others His way. Period.

God is always so awesome even when you can't feel or see it! May God see you through your struggles, and He will!

I love you.
Brennan

Table of Contents

FOREWORD

Brennan is the real deal.

This is the first and foremost fact you need to start with. He has walked the walk and understands what it is like to go from rock bottom to a better life. The struggles he has faced were and are real, but through the power of Jesus and his own determination, he has come into a life that is full and holds the promise of a better tomorrow. I witnessed some of his dark days and was fortunately reunited with him ten years later and able to come alongside him during the last several years as he continues to work on himself and walk out his faith.

This book will inspire you to follow the light as Brennan did to a place of healing and restoration.

Col. Joseph Milner
Retired USAF

INTRODUCTION

Life. This journey we're on. Just as no two souls are alike, no two journeys are alike. Sure, some paths may be similar, but each of us has traveled and is traveling a different path. Unique to each of us, whether filled with heartache, pain, and darkness, wherever you are in your life journey, I'm here to say **don't you dare lose hope**. Through the love and grace of Jesus Christ, your journey through life can ultimately lead to light, fullness, and redemption.

Now let me say right up front, if you think this is a "do this, and everything will be all sunshine and roses" kind of book, you couldn't be further from the truth. Accepting Jesus Christ as your personal Lord and Savior will undoubtedly change your life. It will give you peace and a strength that can only come from Him, but the road—your journey—will still have challenges. The difference is that now facing addictions, dealing with hardships, handling disappointments and loss, and overcoming all of life's challenges become possible.

I'm here to tell you that I've been in the darkness. The darkness has relentlessly sought me out. For the majority of my life, the darkness had such a grip on my life that I felt my only choice was to remove myself from this world. I've experienced abuse from those who should have been protecting me, and I've lived with the anxiety that those types of secrets cause. I've had to find my way with no earthly biological father to look up to and guide my path. I've seen angels and demons and felt the protection of God over my life. I've known the crippling effects that addition causes to the mind, the body, and those who removed themselves from my life because of my addiction.

My story is not your story, and I don't want it to be. What I do want is for my story to serve as your inspiration. The inspiration for whatever you have been through, for whatever you are going through, for whatever you will go through, and you will know that **you can make it**. Let today be the first day of the rest of your life. **I promise you, my brother and my sister, that if you vow not to give up, you can beat whatever is beating you down.** It may not be easy. The devil won't let his stronghold go without a fight. But, with the help of God our Father, you can do this—we can do this together. Will you promise me that? Don't you dare give up.

Salt in the Air

Eagles Nest. I remember the name like it was my own. Not many places or memories from my childhood are pleasant ones, so when a great memory pops, I don't ever want to let it go. That's where Eagles Nest comes in. Eagles Nest is the name of the time share residence I visited a couple of times with my aunt and cousin. It was located on the Florida coast and holds a very special place in my heart.

I recall at least a couple of trips there for our family vacation. I remember white sand, chasing girls, and body boarding along the coast—the smell of the salt air and that glistening white sand as a backdrop. We swam and chucked marshmallows at the manatees. I know what you're thinking, but hey, we were teenage boys, what do you expect! Those times, just hanging with my family, escaping from real life, were some of the best memories of my life.

Everyone needs memories like that, whether you live a blessed life or are struggling just to get by. As my boys grow up, someday, I hope to take them back to the coast so they can experience and create their own Eagles Nest memories. I pray for them daily, and I put my faith and hope in God that my boys will never experience the deep darkness I have, but if someday they find themselves searching for a happy memory, I hope that I can do that for them.

I bet that my aunt and cousin never imagined the long-lasting impact that a simple beach vacation getaway would have on my life. I hope they realize that now.

Dirt in My Cleats

Playing little league is a past-time for young boys and most dream of playing in the big leagues someday. While that wasn't a long-range dream for me, I was blessed with a love and honest talent for the game. And as I've done in everything in my life, I don't believe in giving any less than 100 percent in anything I do. That held true for baseball as well. From the moment I remember putting on the glove and learning to swing in little league to winning the state Legion game, baseball was an integral part in shaping the man I am today. But, while there were certainly fond memories and forever bonds formed, it was a time where drugs and painkillers were already part of my daily routine.

Full Disclosure

I believe in full disclosure and transparency, so here's how the story ends. I'm still standing. Period. What you will discover is that even with my personal relationship with Jesus Christ, the battles and demons didn't stop. Sure, they let up, and the Holy Spirit keeps me safe, but that doesn't mean my battle is over. Each day is a new day, and if yesterday was especially tough, I know when I wake up tomorrow, it's a brand-new day—a day where I get a brand-new start.

In all honesty, my life has been tough, as you'll discover. And through it all, I thought I'd finally found joy in the love of my life. I found my soul mate. We fell deeply in love and were connected in our spirits and our passion for Jesus Christ. It had finally happened for me... For us. Our relationship was different. We'd waited our whole lives and looked forward to living out the rest of our lives together as one happy, blended family.

But then 2020 happened. A little virus took over the world. Political unrest crippled the U.S. Riots... Strained race relations... Job losses... I could go on and on, but as much as I'd like to say those events brought us closer, the opposite is true. I'll go into more detail in that chapter, but as I promised, I want to be transparent. I am not living a life full of sunshine, roses, and butterflies, but I'm standing tall. Because of the grace, love, and forgiveness of my Heavenly Father, I rise and face each day head-on knowing that with His favor, I can live to see another day.

Whatever you are facing. Whether your demons have been chasing you down for decades or just a day, keep reading. Whether your heart is breaking for a close friend or family member because of demons they are trying to manage, keep reading. Whether you just want to read about someone who faced the darkest of times only to use their triumph to help others, keep reading. Most of all, if you just need to know that you are not alone, please keep reading.

Know that I love you and want to see you live the best life possible. I'd love to connect with you and pray for you and with you, if you'd like. I know my story isn't the most uplifting for large periods of time, but it is the story of a fighter... a child of the most high God... and a story of how the darkness will fail when shining the light becomes the focus.

I love you.

Keep reading...

Count it all joy, my brothers, when you meet trials of various kinds, for you know that the testing of your faith produces steadfastness. And let steadfastness have its full effect, that you be perfect and complete, lacking in nothing.

James 1:2–4 (ESV)

CHAPTER ONE

THE EARLY YEARS

What did you want to be when you grew up? Think about that for a minute.

Next question.

Are you presently doing what you thought you would be? If you wanted to be a teacher, are you a teacher? If you wanted to be a professional baseball player, are you still playing baseball? If you wanted to be president, are you going to run for president someday?

It's fun to dream, but let's be real, not many of us get to do what we dreamed of when we were young.

Now I get to answer those questions.

When I was a young boy, there were three things that I remember wanting to be when I grew up. I either wanted to be Superman, a Cop, or in the Military. When you really think about it, each of those careers is the same. While I never was the "real" Superman, I get to play Superman every time I help someone. But the really cool thing is that I was able to achieve not just one but all three of my dreams. You'll read a little later, but I proudly served as a member of our United States Military and also as a law enforcement officer. And since technically both of those positions allowed me to help people... I think I'm going to say I got to be Superman too!

The Innocence of a Child

A very close friend of mine, and the author of this book, shared a story with me about child-like innocence. She and her boyfriend, Mark, liked to go for long drives through the country. They would explore back country roads and just take in the fresh air and scenery of small-town living. On one such drive, they passed a group of elementary children who appeared to be on a school field trip. You may have been on one of those, too, when you were little. The children were sitting on a trailer that was hitched to the back of a large tractor. The trailer bed was lined with bales of hay. The children were, mostly, sitting on the bales, each child clinging to a bright orange pumpkin. Today appeared to be the day they got to visit the farm, go for a bumpy tractor ride to the farmer's field and select their very own pumpkin to take home. The children looked so happy.

Mark, she noticed, was overcome with emotion, but she didn't know why. Tears freely flowed from his eyes. He explained that just the simple sight of those children, innocent and happy, made him equally happy and sad. Sad knowing the type of challenges and battles they will likely face growing up or may even be facing currently in their young lives. Happy because for this one day, this one field trip, they could just be kids. Their only worry for the day would be whether they could pick up their pumpkin and carry it back to the bus when they left. That is the true essence of childhood innocence wrapped into one tractor full of children seen on a beautiful drive through the country. It's no wonder she loved this man. He truly was a kind and genuine soul, even if he was a little rough around the edges.

This innocence that Mark cherished in those children was unfortunately stolen from me. My childhood started out rough and only continued down that path. Is that what caused me to make wrong choices later in life? Choices that would take me to the brink of death and perhaps beyond? It's possible.

You see. The family I grew up around wasn't your typical "Leave it to Beaver" family. It was honestly quite the opposite. My mom, whom you'll see me reference quite often in this book, was my only savior at times. She risked her safety to get us kids out of a bad relationship, and I will be forever grateful to her. These events that took my innocence away were not known to her until much more recently.

My innocence was stolen from me at a time when I was the most vulnerable and from people who were some of the closest to me—people who should have been my advocates and protectors.

I have two sisters and a half-brother. My sisters are a few years older than I am, and my half-brother is about ten years or so younger.

My earliest memories were of a lot of chaos and fighting at home... Fighting between my (birth) father and my mother. He was an alcoholic, and when he drank, he lashed out at anyone who was in his way. My mother received the brunt of his anger and abuse. She would even step in front of us or cling to us just to keep him from physically abusing any of us. I do remember one time where she was holding me, clinging to me with one arm, and waving a butcher knife in the other arm. My father was in a rage, but my mother protected us with everything she had inside of her. She was successful that time—thank you, Jesus! **I love that woman more than anything!**

When he wasn't trying to beat up my mom or my sisters and me, he would go into a violent fit and break windows in our house and bust out windows in our vehicles. Not only was my father physically abusive to my mother, but he was also sexually abusive to her as well. But as you can imagine, the alcoholism also meant he was pretty verbally abusive to all of us. He threatened to kill her if she ever left him.

You'd think that my life would finally be okay once my mom and my father split. I was five at the time. But that wasn't the case.

About a year after my mom and father agreed to divorce, she met the man who would later become my stepdad. I like this one! As with any new relationship, he and my mother would go out on dates, but since I was only about six at the time, I wasn't able to stay home by myself. A female family member stepped in and volunteered to babysit me. On the surface, there was nothing unusual about this. She loved me, or at least that's what she always told me.

What I'm about to share doesn't seem easy to me, and it certainly isn't something that my family likes to hear. It really hasn't even been public-family knowledge until late 2019 or early 2020, I believe. Either way, and as painful as it is for my family, I had to share the good, the bad, and the ugly for me to heal.

This is the bad and the ugly.

Now back to my mom and (future) stepfather's dates. When my mom went on dates with my future stepfather, I was left with a family member. This family member seemed to love spending time with me and accepted any requests to babysit me when asked. It didn't take long for me to figure out why. For the next five years, from the time I was about seven until I was about twelve, she sexually abused me. Honestly, I think the abuse only stopped then because I was old enough to stay home without a babysitter.

It started simple, and she always told me that she loved me. She would touch me in inappropriate ways. I never wanted her to touch me, but she would pull me closer so that I couldn't get away.

One time when we were swimming, she dove under the water and pulled my swimming trunks down so she could touch me. She made it seem like it was all fun and games, but it certainly wasn't fun to me. It got worse. Sometimes it wasn't playful at all. Those times she would just lay on top of me, hold my arms down, and rape me.

This couldn't be what real love was, could it? She would threaten me that she would make sure that I would be in big trouble that she would make sure that I would be in big trouble if I ever even hinted to anyone what was going on to anyone. No one would believe me anyway. And when you're a young boy, when someone tells you that you'll be in big trouble, you believe them, even if you know this can't be right. This went on for close to six years until I was twelve years old.

You would think that this would have been enough trauma to cause lasting damage, but that's just the beginning of what I experienced. In all, there were about six adults who abused me. All were either close family members or friends. I am sure you've heard it said it's usually people close to their victims that end up committing the abuse. People who should be protecting you are instead hurting you in ways in which you will not likely recover. That's what happened to me.

In addition to the female family member, I was abused by four friends of my sisters and the husband of my mom's best friend. The abuse from my family member lasted the longest—six years as I recall. My mom's best friend's husband's abuse was the most severe.

This was during the time that my family member was abusing me when this other abuse happened. He was quite the drug addict, but the other adults in my life seemed to ignore that fact. But one time when he was babysitting me... You are seeing a trend here aren't you? ...Things happened to me whenever these adults were alone with me. This man hurt me so bad that I was bleeding, and he made me take a bath just to clean up the evidence. He raped me from behind, and it was the most painful and scary thing that anyone could experience.

Considering everything I went through with the family member and this man, my sister's friends treated me more like their little experimental science experiment. I was young, and they were quite a bit older than I was.

So, what happened to this family friend? After I "aged out" of her abuse, she seemed to transfer her attention to my younger brother. I do not really know what was going on there, but I heard that she was giving him baths five and six times each night. You can connect the dots here however you would like. My mom found out about these baths, confronted her, and then banned her from ever babysitting either of us ever again. That was the last I saw her, but the damage had already been done.

Until very recently, I had held these secrets to myself. It wasn't until the 700 Club approached me about doing a story about my life that I realized I needed to share my experiences with my family. The last thing I wanted to do was to have them blindsided. They needed to hear it from me.

My mom had always wondered why her best friend stopped visiting and cut her off from all communication. It never made sense, but slowly now, the realization was setting in. As a mother, hearing the trauma that I went through was almost too much to bear. Hearing who the abusers were was like experiencing death. But then there was a death, wasn't there? The death of my childhood. The death of my innocence. The death of my trust in adults.

My mother and biological father ended up officially divorcing when I was a young teenager. Even after their divorce, and because he was my father, I spent time with him on occasion. These were not joyous father-son bonding weekends, I can assure you of that.

These times were still filled with the sounds and images of abuse, only this time the abuse was concentrated on his (then) girlfriend. He was still drinking heavily, and when he came home, all bets were off as to how he would act. The verbal abuse was a given, but he would also physically abuse her and even forcibly (and violently) rape her in plain sight.

He would apologize to her and tell her that he was sorry and loved her. How could this be love? Could it really be? I mean, the people who abused me said they loved me too. It was the only example of love that I had seen from some people, but it just did not seem like this was how it was supposed to be. I know my mom loved me, and so did (her new boyfriend) Jeff, but the love I was shown from others should not be something experienced in relation to abuse and pain. Would I ever experience a different type of love, or was this all there was?

They would eventually separate, but the visual and emotional scars from my dad and his girlfriend that I carried with me have never left.

I mentioned my mom's new boyfriend earlier. Well, they hit it off and decided to get married. I now had a stepdad. We got along well, and he made (and still makes) my mom very happy, but he wasn't really the type to openly express his love to me or just give me a hug out of the blue. I think I needed that after all I'd been through, so since I never got it, it was almost as if another man was withholding the love and support that I didn't even realize I craved.

I do have some great memories of growing up with my stepfather. The ones that stuck out the most to me were when we'd drive up to go hunting in the woods together or to the lake for tubing and boating. In my younger days, it was always fun to see him dress up as Santa Claus on Christmas! As I grew older and we grew closer, we'd work out together. Now that I'm an adult, it's great just to spend time riding our Harley's together.

Being a father is an important job, just like being a good mother is. But my (biological) father was not a loving one. It was like I had the wrong father—a father from Satan.

As I write and share this story of the dark beginning of my growing up, I am grateful that I have my Heavenly Father in my life. He protects and gives me support and everlasting love with each and every moment of my life. He is the father who is always there for me. The Father I can confide in, the Father I can trust. The Father who ***only*** has my best interest at heart. The Father who will ***never*** leave me or hurt me.

Do you know this Heavenly Father?

Keep reading...

Interlude of Innocence...

I know I just shared how my abuse started and continued through most of my youth, but I did have moments where I was just a kid doing "kid things". It wasn't all bad.

Elementary School

I bet you would never believe it, but I was a little troublemaker. I can just picture my mom nodding her head without hesitation at this statement. Come to think of it, I don't think I've quite grown out of this stage. Is it too late?

I was the class clown. I would talk back to the teacher and do things just for attention. In second grade, I also got kicked off the bus! As I think back to these days, I imagine I used humor and laughter to mask the demons I was fighting in my real life. I guess if I was laughing or deferring attention to other things or events, no one would notice the sheer pain and confusion I was dealing with for real. Could you even imagine the tormenting I would go through, both at home and with my friends, if they knew the abuse I was suffering?

As I grew a little older, I remember hanging out with my grandfather, and I'd get to be a normal young boy for a while. I'd chase toads, and we'd go camping. There was something about being in the woods or near a lake. To this day, I find myself drawn to being in nature, admiring God's beauty, and reflecting on life.

But you know my camping trips weren't all that innocent. Leaving the cooler unattended was never a good thing. So, by the time I was around ten years old, I was already stealing beers from the cooler.

I remember summers at the beach. Two trips, in particular, stand out in my mind. This beach we would go to in Florida was where we'd go for a family vacation. The sand was so white, and the girls were pretty. I would act cool with my skimboard and even remember swimming with the manatees.

If only I could go back to that innocence.

My biological dad died when I was thirteen. I had been out with a friend and returned home to find a law enforcement officer at my house. He's the one who told me, and from that moment, my abuse stopped.

One thing you'll learn about me is that I am not a quitter. When I set my mind on something, I go after it 100 percent. Sports was no different. I started with baseball and, if I don't say so myself, was pretty good at it. I enjoyed pitching and playing left field. When I was about fourteen or so, we went to the State Legion game, and we won, thanks in part to the one-hitter that I pitched.

Given my drive for perfection and my goal of internalizing any and all pain from the abuse, you know that I couldn't be just a one-sport athlete. So, I added football to my extracurricular activities! If I remember correctly, I started around middle school (which is later than most kids nowadays). With a full-contact sport like football, there are bound to be injuries. And with someone with my physique and drive to be the best running and cornerback there ever was, you can be sure there were injuries on my horizon. But, with injuries come pain medication. We would soon find out just how fast addiction to those pain medications would take hold. I was fourteen.

Keep reading...

CHAPTER TWO

ADDICTION TAKES HOLD

You can have the grandest or even the simplest of plans, but then life just seems to happen, and our journey begins. We can only hope to buckle the seatbelt and hang on for the ride.

Life is funny like that.

Author Unknown

It was 2001, and I'd just injured myself playing football. I had a torn rotator cuff, and the pain was excruciating. A friend gave me some pills to try for pain. Those pills were Vicodin. They worked. It didn't take many for me to be hooked. Once my injury was healed and I was cleared to play football again, I started using these pills before every game. I figured that if they could take the pain away, I could play that much harder. They were just pain pills; how harmful could they be, right? I was a teenager. I was thirteen. I was practically a man. I could quit anytime I wanted.

This was the first time I had ever taken any pain medication, and it was like nothing I'd ever experienced before. This was my introduction to Vicodin, and I was instantly in love. Not only did it help me with my injury pain, but when I took it, all of the other pain—physical and emotional—from my abuse went away as well.

When there weren't enough pills left. I didn't know what to do, so I rummaged through my mother's dresser drawers in search of her pain pills. She received the pills to help with a previous injury, and I remembered that she didn't take them that much. Of course, I didn't have a problem. Or so I thought. I could still quit at any time, right?

The pharmacy kept refilling my prescription, so my supply continued. I could tell that I was starting to rely on the pills more and more to escape from all of my pain. How could I get more pills? It was easy. Just change the number. I changed the pill count from thirty to ninety on the bottles, and it actually worked. Now my supply was set! It's at this point that I started "popping pills".

Do you have a song that, when you hear it, instantly it takes you back to a moment? Maybe it's a song that takes you back to your first kiss or first intimate moment. From the first chords, you are transported back to that moment in time. Maybe it's a song that was played at the funeral of a loved one or a song playing on the radio when you drove your first car off the lot. I'd be willing to bet you are thinking of that song at this very moment.

My song is *Rooster* by the group *Alice in Chains*, and it's not a song that brings happy memories. This is the song that was playing when my abuse and addiction to narcotics was taken to the point of no return.

Fast Forward Just One Year

I was fourteen and was attending a birthday party. It was a casual campout with a bonfire. Very chill. I was hanging out in a car with a friend listing to music. My friend was expressing his condolences at losing my dad when he showed me a 20 milligram Oxycontin pill. He then began to crush it up and invited me to just snort it off of the CD case. "Don't think about it, just snort it," he said. So that's what I did.

And with that, my addiction was now on an entirely new path—A dangerous and destructive path.

The high I felt was like nothing I'd ever experienced before. To the backdrop of the song, euphoria kicked in, and I almost thought I was God incarnate. The feeling I got from popping a couple of Vicodin was like taking baby aspirin compared to my new love. Oxycontin and I would embark on our new relationship.

By the summer of 2002, I was dabbling in other drugs. Mushrooms. Cocaine. LSD. But, no Heroin, yet.

My friends and I would go on a walk every day—sometimes more than one time a day. You see, when I took it, any of it, if I stayed still, I would get physically sick—hugging the porcelain god kind of sick. So, I would take it and then just stroll around. Sometimes alone with my thoughts, and other times with my group of friends who also used. There were six of us, and those guys were the only ones entrusted with that secret.

This went on for about four years. Most of my friends were successful in stopping anytime they tried, but I was not so lucky. I was a full-blown addict and unable to stop. Additionally, because my highs also masked the pain from my past, I found that I needed more and more drugs.

My mother had suspicions that I had been taking her pills, but since she rarely used them herself, she just figured she miscounted. She only refilled them every six months, so it was easy to lose track of how many there really were. Eventually, however, she started to keep track of them more closely and confronted me when some came up missing. Of course, I denied using any of them. Time passed, and the topic never came up again.

When I was seventeen, I had all four wisdom teeth extracted. My mom took me to the oral surgeon, and after the surgery, he gave me a script for thirty Vicodin. My mom had to make a stop at Walgreen's to pick up gauze, and while she was inside, I changed the script from thirty to eighty. Yup, I thought I was a genius and would never get caught. My mom then stopped at the pharmacy to drop off my script while I waited in the car. The pharmacist had pulled my mom aside and threatened her with calling the authorities for tampering with a prescription. He told her it was a federal crime. She knew the workers at the pharmacy well as we lived in a small town where everyone knew everyone! Needless to say, when mom came back to the car, she was livid and very embarrassed. Of course, I denied doing it, and again... life went on.

Shortly before I was eighteen, I realized that I had a real problem and needed help. I called my sister to see if she had any advice, and she was instrumental in my admission to Genesis Treatment Facility in Milwaukee so that I could detox. I made the call to my mom to tell her I was addicted, and although she was devasted, I don't think she realized we were on the start of a long and brutal road. She was proud that I took it upon myself to seek treatment, and I believe she thought all would be good and back to normal that after this week. Unfortunately, that wasn't the case, and the nightmare would continue for years. The true nightmare was just beginning.

When I was released, mom took me to a suboxone doctor in Fond du Lac. We were hopeful that counseling would be the answer. However, the answer was that I would need long-term treatment and meds that would cost over $1000 a month... FOR LIFE! My mom was devasted yet again but willing to do whatever was needed to save me.

I came back home and tried to get my life "back to normal" but struggled. I was angry, resentful, and belligerent and would miss work constantly. I was very hard to be around.

I knew others would never understand my love, drugs, and me, so I kept things hidden, especially from my parents, or so I thought. In one dramatic moment, my stepdad found a safe tucked away in a drawer. It was filled with syringes, steroids, and various pills. It was at that moment that he gave me an ultimatum that either I stopped using drugs or I was no longer welcome to live under his roof. I was told that I needed to either get out, find something productive to do—other than drugs, of course—or join the military... Something... Anything other than destroying my life by using drugs.

So with that, I made my choice. I enlisted in the Air Force a few weeks later.

Keep reading...

CHAPTER THREE

SERVING MY COUNTRY

Off we go into the wild blue yonder,
Climbing high into the sun;
Here they come zooming to meet our thunder,
At 'em, boys, Give 'er the gun! (Give er the gun now!)
Down we dive, spouting our flame from under,
Off with one helluva roar!
We live in fame or go down in flame. Hey!
Nothing will stop the U.S. Air Force!
Minds of men fashioned a crate of thunder,
Sent it high into the blue;
Hands of men blasted the world asunder;
How they lived God only knew! (God only knew then!)
Souls of men dreaming of skies to conquer,
Gave us wings, ever to soar!
With scouts before And bombers galore. Hey!
Nothing'll stop the U.S. Air Force![1]

1 "AFNOA - Air Force Song (Old and New) by Major Robert Crawford, 1939," American Airforce Navigator Observer Association [AFNOA], n.d., https://www.afnoa.org/afsong.html.

I was in the eighth grade. It was in History class, I believe, when my suddenly-somber-appearing teacher wheeled the T.V. cart into our room. They turned on the television to allow us to see what was transpiring in our world. A day our nation, and our world for that matter, would forever be changed. The date was September eleventh.

Like anyone alive in our country on that day, I, too, remember the exact moment I learned we were under attack in America. I remember exactly where I was, and it pierced me to the core.

At first, I was in shock. I mean, who wasn't. What kind of crazy person (or people) would fly an airplane into a building? And, not just that, but an airplane full of people into a building full of unsuspecting people just starting their day... as if it was just another typical morning. This day was anything but typical. As the news wore on, my emotions turned from shock and fear to full-blown anger. This was my country they were attacking. These were American lives they were destroying.

Hijackers took control of 4 planes that day.

Close to 3,000 American's died, including:

NYC Firefighters

NYC Police Officers

NYC Port Authority Officers

Pentagon workers

Trade Center Workers
Innocent bystanders and passengers on:
American Airlines Flight 11
United Airlines Flight 175
American Airlines Flight 77
United Airlines Flight 93[2]

From the first attack on the World Trade Center tower to the moment both towers fell, just 102 minutes passed.[3] Nineteen hijackers had just crippled the America that I knew and loved.[4]

It was from that very moment, I knew I would enroll in the military when I was able. So, in the midst of my addiction, my stepfather's ultimatum set that plan in motion. At the age of eighteen, I graduated early and went to visit my local Armed Services Recruiter. As is still the case, all new "potential" recruits take the ASVAB aptitude test to figure out what branch and job best suits their skill set. It was determined that my best match would be an aircraft mechanic since I scored a 96 on the exam. So, I signed up.

---

2 Jocelyn Fiset, "9/11 by the Numbers: Victims, Hijackers, Aftermath, and More Facts about September 11, 2001," ABC7 San Francisco, 2021, https://abc7news.com/911-september-11-victims-facts-about-how-many-planes-were-hijacked-on/11006480/.
3 "On 9/11, 102 Minutes That Changed America," Insider, 2016, https://www.businessinsider.com/afp-on-911-102-minutes-that-changed-america-2016-9.
4 Fiset, 2021.

It Was April 2008

The training was to begin in several months, but I could not wait. I equally couldn't wait to leave my home and start my military career. I knew that if I stayed home much longer, I would probably either end up dead from an overdose or killed by some unfortunate event. I just had to get on with this next chapter of my life.

As luck would have it, or maybe it was by some divine intervention, a position within the Military Police opened up with a start date of just two weeks. So, rather than wait months for the aircraft mechanic position, I decided to accept this job. I shipped out to start Basic Training at Lackland AFB in San Antonio, Texas, just a few weeks later.

It Was Now May 2008

I'll admit, as excited as I was to finally start a new part of my life and help defend this country I loved so much, I wasn't in a good mindset when I started basic training. I had already been to detox but knew I was going to have to deal with my addiction battle on my own. I started my detox.

Basic training seemed to be what I exactly needed. It proved to be an outlet for all of my anxiety and abuse. I finished basic training with the second overall (highest) score for fitness standards since 1947. That's something I'm incredibly proud of, and I believe my record score still stands to this day. Don't hold me to that; I may have to confirm. And, as it turns out, I was a pretty good marksman as well. As a result of my shooting skills, I was invited to attend sniper school. I had found my niche and was sent to my first station in California at Vandenberg AFB, and within the first month, I was considered a "super troop". I was put on patrol and assigned to police one. I was on my way. I was popular, dedicated, sober, off drugs, and on my way to being quickly advanced in rank.

It Was June 2008

I had pushed myself beyond what I even thought was capable, and it showed. I was getting noticed. I was a new man, unrecognizable to my former self for once in my life.

At this point, I volunteered for deployment. I really wish I could share with you what I saw, experienced, and what my mission was, but I am unable to due to a confidentiality agreement currently in force. But I can tell you this... In America, we live in a great country; we should be proud and ***never*** take for granted the freedoms and lifestyles we are afforded. So, whether you are at your peak, in your valley, or somewhere in between, just know that there are people in this world who would sacrifice their life to have a taste of life we many times take for granted.

I graduated from my Special Forces training in September 2008, and the very next month, I received orders that I would be deploying to Iraq. Unfortunately, I would miss my sister's wedding in December that year.

I came home from that deployment for a short two weeks in April 2009 to visit and spend time with my family. I'd volunteered for a 365-day tour—a full-year deployment—and was home to train prior to heading out on a new deployment.

I returned to California for this deployment training and decided to head out for a night on the town with some other Airmen friends of mine. I wanted to celebrate my twenty-first birthday. That night my life changed trajectories yet again. This time was different in ways I wasn't expecting. I stepped outside the bar just to smoke a cigarette when I was approached and jumped by several men. They punched me in the jaw with brass knuckles, threw me to the curb, and continued to stomp me into unconsciousness. I was one of four others who were innocently and violently attacked that night. We later discovered the beatings were part of a local gang initiation.

The police never charged anyone for this crime.

I suffered a crushed double mandible, a broken ear socket, and a traumatic brain injury. My mom flew out as soon as she received word and found me in the hospital bed hooked up to morphine. Again, she was devasted, not just to see me so beaten, but that I was also on a morphine drip, which she knew could be the start of a nightmare after working so hard to get clean and enlist. I had excelled at so much in the military, and now this!

I found out later that my mom had secretively talked with the surgeon and asked him not to prescribe any narcotics, and he reassured her that he could prescribe other non-narcotic meds, but it wouldn't do a whole lot for relieving my pain. She didn't care as that pain was way easier to handle than becoming addicted again, especially when in the military, but the talk didn't do anything. The day I was released, they sent me home with several different narcotics to use. Then on top of that, I also had to see my Air Force physician and was prescribed even more! Nine meds in all!

Ativan 2 mg

Fentanyl patches

Fentanyl suckers

Liquid codeine

Liquid Vicodin

Lorazepam

Morphine

Oxycontin30 mg

Valium

My mom stayed for about ten days to take care of me. I barely remember her even being with me as I was so jacked up on meds. It's even hard today for her to talk about that experience as she saw first-hand how the Air Force handled things, well maybe I should say, how they didn't handle things. She remembers answering my phone several times for me, and it was the pharmacy leaving messages that I had more fentanyl patches to pick up. She called and told them that I didn't want or need anymore, but the calls continued. She had to leave to go back to Wisconsin to work her business and asked the other airman and a sergeant to please take me to my appointments and help me through as I was on so many meds and shouldn't be driving. They never helped me, and I ended up having to drive myself to my appointments.

For six long months, I was stuck in my room. I was physically unable to do anything, let alone perform any duties related to my job. I fell into a deep, dark depression. My mouth remained wired shut. The depression, the endless supply of pills and narcotics, brought me to such a low point. I knew I needed help. That's when I decided to speak with my First Sergeant.

I explained to him that I had a problem and that I was overtaking my medications. I told him that they had prescribed way too many medications, and that scared me. I did not want to slip back into the addiction that had almost killed me. I was stuck in my treatment room and unable to travel due to my injury. I was crying out for his help. He agreed and immediately asked me to go on a ride with him to get the help that I needed. Praise Jesus; someone was finally listening to me.

I was wrong.

Instead, my First Sergent took me straight to the OSI Office. This was the Office of Special Investigations, and instead of the help, I thought I was getting, I was interrogated and confronted on my medication abuse. Wait... I was just asking for help but instead was being criminalized for no reason. They held me for more than twenty-four hours with no food or water while they drilled me with question after question.

You've probably seen those police or investigative shows on T.V. where they interrogate the witness or suspected criminal in such a manner and for so long that the person ultimately will do anything to make it stop. They'll confess to crimes they didn't commit or admit to things just so the harassment will stop. That's where it ended with me.

In order to be released and go back home, all I needed to do was write a statement—with the information they requested in it, of course. I had to admit that I was abusing my drugs, and so that's what I did. But it didn't stop there. Not only did they want me to confess that I was abusing my drugs, but they also wanted me to admit that I was giving my medications to other people. In that moment of weakness and because I desperately wanted out of this situation, I wrote that statement as well. I just couldn't sign it. I was finally released and returned to try and salvage my military service. I soon learned that was going to be easier said than done.

I returned to base and entered a living nightmare. In my mind anyway. I received retaliation almost immediately. The harassment and embarrassment were intense and unfounded. I had my badge and stripes ripped off of my uniform in public. I was made to sing the Air Force song to incoming flights of recruits on command, made to work extra and in jobs that were well beneath my stature and duties. It was a horrible time where I do not think I could have been treated any worse, and I hadn't even been found guilty of anything—yet.

After what seemed like an eternity, I was finally offered treatment for my newly acquired addiction. I was offered a twenty-eight day treatment at the Hemet Valley Recovery Center in Hemet, California. Twenty-eight days. I knew I could do this. It certainly would work better than the measly three-day detox I did when I was eighteen. But due to the ineptitude of my counselor, who always had something else more important to deal with, I was forced to stay 112 days. Are you kidding me? I was powerless, but it was about to get worse, and I had no idea what was ahead.

The drug addiction was finally resolved, only to open up another issue. Are you ready for this one? On the day that I returned to my base, I was escorted to my First Sergeant's office and charged with six Federal Charges for abusing each of the individual medications that I had. These were the medications that were prescribed to me. Altogether, the convictions for these charges could lead to eighteen years in prison. I was being court marshaled.

I secured a lawyer with the help of my sister, who loaned me the $20,000 for lawyer fees, and we began the fight. My lawyer, by the way, was none other than a very powerful attorney who worked on President Trump's team. If you are going in for the fight of a lifetime, you might as well get the best.

Meanwhile, I headed back and tried to keep my nose clean and continue to work, but this grew increasingly difficult due to all the harassment I continued to endure. People would sit outside my dorm and listen to my every word. I was threatened by an agent at a gas station. He came up to me for no apparent reason and said that I'd better watch my back, or he'd find a way to make me disappear. I was being treated like I was some drug lord when in reality, all I was taking was my prescribed medications. The medications they were prescribing me. It just so happened they were severely over medicating me.

My mom flew out to support me, and we now prepared to go to court. It was a circus. People were thrown out of the courtroom, including the First Sergeant and other agents who had not told the truth.

My lawyer pulled a rabbit out of his hat and put me on the stand. I was finally able to tell my story. I was nervous, but I knew I was doing the right thing. I admitted to abusing my medications.

The courtroom scene was similar to that famous scene from A Few Good Men. You know the scene where the character played by Tom Cruise is cross-examining the character played by Jack Nicholson? Tom Cruise yells that he wants the truth, and then in one of the most famous of movies lines, Jack Nicholson yells back, "You can't handle the truth." Okay, maybe my experience wasn't quite that dramatic, but it's just as impactful—just on a different scale.

Maybe it was all orchestrated by the Holy Spirit, but one of the agents became overwhelmed with emotion, and guilt I imagine. The agent who was just on the stand flat out lied. This agent then took the stand and, speaking through his tears, admitted I had requested a lawyer, that they had indeed been harassing me, and he really didn't think I had done anything wrong. Wow, you can imagine my surprise! I think I held my breath the entire time he gave his testimony, wondering what else he was going to say.

In part due to this brave agent's testimony, it was determined that the OSI had, in fact, lied and brought in false witnesses—three of them to be exact—who later admitted they didn't even know who I was. When the jury came back from deliberation, the judge read that I had been acquitted of all charges. He also said this was a complete waste of time and a false court martial.

They promised to get me to a new base so I could move forward in a fresh environment. Since the judges presiding over cases are not tied to any one base, I was confident that I received a fair, unbiased trial. The very next day, I was processed with an honorable discharge but with a drug abuse notation on my reenlistment code. This was a death sentence. It meant I was no longer able to do anything and made it look like I was still in the wrong. So, essentially everything I'd just been fighting to not have happen, just happened.

After this happened, I no longer had medical insurance, so the pain I was still experiencing on a daily basis wasn't able to be managed. As a result, I became rather ill. Not to mention that when you are cut off from medicine cold turkey, it's incredibly difficult to adapt. And, as you remember, I wasn't on just one medication. If you remember anything about me, you know that I'm going to find a way, any way to make my pain go away. I learned that the only way to keep the pain manageable was to start using again. This time my drug of choice happened to be opiates and heroin. Heroin isn't something you walk to the nearest drug store and pick up over the counter. Heroin can only be found on the streets, and I knew where to find it. And just like that, my addiction took hold again. Only this time, I wasn't the only one who was being hurt. I was married and had a child on the way.

Keep reading...

CHAPTER FOUR

ADDICTION AND HOMELESSNESS ON THE WAY TO ROCK BOTTOM

Do not be anxious about anything, but in everything by prayer and supplication with thanksgiving let your requests be made known to God. And the peace of God, which surpasses all understanding, will guard your hearts and your minds in Christ Jesus.

Philippians 4:6–7 (ESV)

When I was in the Hemet Valley Recovery Center, I met JoAnne. I was twenty-two.

When we first met, she already had two children from a previous relationship, and we were about to add another one to that mix. The very first time we slept together, JoAnne, or rather, we became pregnant. This was obviously very new in our relationship, but against my family's opinions, I chose to marry JoAnne. I wanted to try at least to do things the right way.

Shortly after Landen was born, Isaiah followed. These boys are my world!

Back from Iraq, I was fighting my losing battle with the Air Force. With nowhere to go, I decided to move my little family back to Wisconsin. Only this time, my addiction was in full swing. (Remember my comment from the previous chapter about opiates and heroin). Just four years from attending the recovery center and meeting JoAnne, I was already homeless. I know what you're thinking. Surely I had to have had a home somewhere, right? I did have a home—under a bridge in Milwaukee. My rehab, relapse, and getting clean cycle repeated itself for a little while until things really started to spiral out of control in my life.

In a period of three years or so, I was in this downward spiral. In addition to the cycle of rehabs and relapses I previously mentioned, I was arrested on a gun possession charge, charged with a switchblade in my glovebox, and an assault. I was living out of my car during this time and had lost contact with my boys. I was arrested numerous times and just couldn't seem to get out of this downward spiral. But was I even trying? If I remember correctly, I think I've been in more than a dozen rehab facilities, and I've been homeless almost ten times in four different states.

I almost died, and the devil was there to catch me. The devil or one of his demons was always nearby. On one occasion, I developed a serious blood infection because of the bad stuff I was using. I ended up in the hospital for three months. I developed septic shock. It was so bad that I almost lost my arm, but luckily that did not happen. But I did have to learn how to walk and even talk again. The doctors tried to prepare my mom that I may never make it. They were expecting that I might die from this.

While I spent most of those three months alone with my thoughts, there were others in there as well. Nurses, yes, but in this case, I'm referring to demons. Now, I know what you're thinking but stay with me here.

This particular demon had been tormenting me and raping me my entire life to this point—a female demon, but with no feminine features to note. Brown, raisin textured skin, and razor-sharp pointy teeth like puppies have—the kind that could pierce your skin with the smallest of bites.

The face remained hidden from me, but I could make out other details. Her eyes were like black stones, and her nails were long and ragged. She'd just stand there... staring... piercing my soul with thoughts of self-harm manifesting in me.

I blocked "her" out as much as I could, but when you're alone in a hospital room with nothing to do, for as long as I was in there, my mind races and my thoughts change. The voice and thoughts of self-harm began to take hold. After about two and a half months into my three months stay in the hospital, I told my nursing staff that I wanted to have some privacy. This was something they were hesitant to give me for the duration of my stay, but I insisted. I told them I wanted to take a shower, and because I'd grown stronger, they agreed to let me do this. They had no idea what I was planning to do.

I grabbed a belt strap from my bed, hung it from the showerhead in an attempt to take my own life. I'd written a simple suicide note for my boys:

I'm sorry, I love you.

I stepped up on the chair, closed my eyes, and all I remember was letting go of the showerhead. I immediately blacked out and felt I was teleported to some distant land.

I found myself kneeling on a peaceful, beautiful, secluded beach covered in the softest of white sand. I didn't recognize His voice at that moment, but God spoke to me. He placed His hand on my head, and the sensation of warm honey being poured on me overcame me as He spoke. I heard Him say that everything is going to be okay.

I'm not sure how long I blacked out before the nurses came in to rescue me, but I hadn't even fallen off the chair. I may have been out a few seconds, minutes, or even longer. I was just slumped over. I experienced incredible amounts of pain as if I was hosting all the pain in the world in my now limp body.

I had been very angry that day. With the demon standing in the corner, it left a very unsettling aura in the room. Although no one could see it, no one wanted to sit or go near that corner of the room. It was as if they could sense the presence of something evil without knowing what they were avoiding.

That day was the culmination of many other recent days from that hospital day. I was angry at everyone. I was telling everyone to "screw" themselves—from the nurses to the doctors to the aids who were just trying to help me. I'd had enough of them, of everyone, of my life. I'd been on a lot of pain medicines, and when the doctors took me off of them, they were not gentle about it. I was cut-off cold turkey, and I didn't appreciate that one bit.

I did not die that day as much as that demon hoped that I would. But what happened that day also wasn't enough to scare me clean. I still managed to relapse again after this. One thing I can say is that after that failed suicide attempt and my meeting with God, the demon was no longer standing in the corner of the room. It was gone.

After this event, I was sent into a different type of facility to address my mental state since obviously trying to kill myself meant I was a bit unstable. You think?

This first facility was in Northern Virginia, and when it didn't work out, I was sent to a new facility. I believe this one was in Arizona. I ended up being kicked out of that facility because, well, I couldn't keep myself clean. That pattern continued for a while until I was back in Arizona, homeless and living on the street. Because I hadn't received the help that I needed, I was using, again. This homelessness lasted about a year.

As I think about that statement, "I hadn't received the help that I needed," wow, how could I have been so self-serving?. I've already been to treatment center upon treatment center, and in each one of those centers, there was someone trying to help me. Together with my pride and unwillingness to submit to any of these resources given to me, perhaps I needed something different. Maybe I needed a rehabilitation that was not so formal. Could it be that I just needed to find Jesus? Could it really be that simple? That one man could be the answer I was seeking. The answer that I just hadn't found yet.

•••

You've heard the expression, you don't know what someone is going through unless you walk a mile in their shoes... Imagine being an addict. Every fiber of your being is longing for the next hit, the next high, to ease the pain. People don't realize what happens when you give in to your addiction—when you let your addiction control you.

While I was relapsing or strung out on heroin—or any other drug for that matter—I had no ability to function as a normal adult. I couldn't hold a job, that's for sure. And with no job, I had no "honest" form of money coming in. I had no place to stay, so for two years, I lived out of my car.

Sure, I had friends and acquaintances who offered to let me sleep on their couches or in a spare place in their homes, but I was way too proud to stoop to needing their charity. I'd rather suffer through it however I could manage. If that meant sleeping in my car, then so be it. I slept in my car. If it meant that I needed to sleep on the street or even on a park bench, I slept on the street or a park bench. For the period of about two years, between 2012 and 2014, it was so bad that I lived out of my car almost exclusively.

So, without a job, in addition to no money for food or a place to live, it also meant that getting the needles I needed to shoot up were hard to get as well. Of course, the needles were the necessity to my drug habit, so I did what everyone else seemed to do. I stole them. Sometimes I got caught. Sometimes I didn't. When I was caught, I ended up going to jail.

I would again try treatment centers, but it seemed that I always left unchanged and relapsed immediately upon leaving. I decided that treatment centers and whatever their method to "fix" me was not working for me.

•••

JoAnne had somehow stayed with me through all of this, or rather not really by my side, but hadn't officially left me yet. After leaving the hospital from the infection that should have killed me, I went to Arkansas for a few months and then headed back to Wisconsin, where this next relapse officially began. Jo-Anne wasn't happy, but I didn't care. I was strung out for about the next nine months before hitting rock bottom back in California at Huntington Beach.

I proceeded to try several more recovery centers, but they never seemed to work for me. I headed next to the Grand Canyon, where I was homeless again, before returning back to Wisconsin. I connected again with my mom this time, and she had one of those "come to Jesus" type conversations with me. The ultimatum was pretty much that I needed to straighten up my act together. Well... duh! But how?

You can't just tell an addict they need help and expect them to say, "Why didn't I think about that?" It has to be time for them. They have to be in a position where they want to get help for themselves just as badly as you want it for them.

I returned to California and had my first encounter with God at the Sea Cliff Recovery Center in California. I wish I could tell you this was where all the planets aligned for me, and I lived happily ever after, but I can't. I ultimately relapsed again.

Keep reading...

CHAPTER FIVE

SPIRITUAL WARFARE

The actual translation of demon means "replete with wisdom" connoting that the demons were highly knowledgeable creatures, evident in their knowledge of an individual's secretive sins. Demons were fallen angels who followed Lucifer from his expulsion from heaven by God to hell[5].

The devil attacks those with the most power to affect the Kingdom of God.

If that's the case, I most certainly must have a mission to serve my Heavenly Father before me!

In the movie *The Sixth Sense*, the young boy famously states, "I see dead people." There's a huge and unexpected twist at the end of the movie, but I'm not going to give that away for you here.

In my case, I've seen demons or demonic figures. I've been

5 "Shalom Headlines," Facebook, 2020, https://www.facebook.com/shalomheadlines/posts/demonic-world-and-how-its-work-the-term-demon-is-derived-from-the-greek-word-dai/121101616298139/.

attacked and followed by Satan and his demons from when I was just a little boy.

I shared with you the witch demon that was with me in my hospital room. This was the first time I'd ever come face to face with that one. She (using that term loosely) had been tormenting me since I started getting abused at the age of five. Coincidence?

There Were More

During a stay at a group home in my younger days, I remember a black blob-type demon. Anytime someone would raise their voice in the facility, it would grow in energy. It would get so close that I could feel it, but it wasn't just present when I was awake. This demon would paralyze me when I was dreaming. It would rape me in my dreams, and I remember it injecting me with disease.

Then there was Crystal. She was a girl I had been dating for a while. Did you ever have one of those relationships where after it's over, you wonder, "What was I even thinking?" Well, this was one of those times. I believe that she was a present for me from the Devil. This was right after I had gotten baptized, so the timing is pretty suspect. Here's why I believe that.

First, Crystal was practicing witchcraft, and I'd even witnessed her levitating. Secondly, the evil, demon woman returned. I was sitting at the dining table in the kitchen one evening, and this creature appeared on the other side of the plate glass sliding doors. It initially started out staring like when it inhabited my hospital room, but then it just stood there banging its head against the glass—continually banging its head against the glass. The glass never even cracked. The demon figure just continued banging their head on the glass violently and very rapidly. Thirdly, I heard voices telling me to kill myself with an extension cord. The voices stopped when a Christian song just began to play without prompting.

These next two events are just more in line with why I think she was from the Devil. Not to take any of the importance and fear from the first events, but, well, you'll see.

Fourthly, one day, there was a knock at the door. I opened it to find two Jehovah's Witness's asking if they could come in and share the good news with me. I let them in, but when we sat at the kitchen table, it was clear they were not of this world. The female could not stop sobbing. It was as if she had no control over her body or her emotions. But the male, well, he was certainly not of this world. His eyes were flames. Yes, you read that correctly. He had flames for eyes.

Lastly, this one is my favorite. Her name was Gail God, and she was a good visitor. She was a visitor sent to save me from certain harm. On this day in 2017, I was heading to a bar. It was closed. This was odd because this bar was never closed. But, for some reason, it was closed this day. As I was in the parking lot, a car with Missouri license plates approached me. There was a woman driving, all alone. She spoke to me immediately, without any hesitation or trepidation. Think about it, a sixty-seven-year-old woman driving alone, enters a bar parking lot, and immediately approaches a young male, who is also by himself.

Anyway, she yells over to me, "They're closed! You shouldn't be here anyway."

She invites me to go with her for a cup of coffee, and I say yes. I know what you're wondering... *Who's the dumb one, you know?* But stick with me here. As we're talking, she starts telling me about her son. His name was also Brennan; he was twenty-six and a heroin addict. Cue the goosebumps! I think all the hair on my arms was standing on edge. She went on to say that he was thrown off of a parking garage and almost died from his injuries.

We talked for about three hours when she just abruptly left. She was wearing a jean jacket and blue jeans, and as she was leaving, I saw her adjusting fluffy white wings on her back. I followed her out to the parking lot to say goodbye, but her car just disappeared as if into thin air.

We had exchanged telephone numbers during our conversation and talked a few times. Her number was then disconnected.

I continued to hear voices, and they escalated quite a bit as my thirtieth birthday approached. Everyday voices would put suicidal thoughts into my head. But each day, I started to gain strength. I was beginning to become prophetic.

Sometime after this, as my ability to prophecy began to increase, I began to see signs. One on such occasion, I was visiting my sister. We were looking through the Bible when the words began to illuminate.

> *He will cover you with his feathers, and under his wings you will find refuge; his faithfulness will be your shield and rampart.*
>
> **Psalm 91:4 (NIV)**

> *The Bible associates feathers with holiness and purity as embodied in angels which are the purest and most divine creatures that God ever made. The importance of feathers is linked to them being able to mobilize the angels so that they can play their important role in spreading love and peace.*[6]

Do you believe in angels? I believe in an angel by the name of Gail.

Keep reading...

6 Sam Ellis, Sam, "What Do Feathers Symbolize In The Bible?" Catholics & Bible, 2020, https://catholicsbible.com/what-do-feathers-symbolize-in-the-bible/.

CHAPTER SIX
A MOTHER'S LOVE

I love my mom more than words can possibly express. What she has been through in her life and how she shines for the love of God is truly an inspiration to me. I don't know what I would do without her.

When I first approached my mom about contributing to my book, she was admittedly a bit nervous. I know I've put her through a lot, but more than that, it's hard to put yourself out there for everyone to see. People can be mean, that's putting it mildly based on our world today, and it's easier just not to say anything. Perhaps more the case is that a lot of what I've shared in this book is really new information. My mom only recently found out about most of what I went through with the abuse. That's a really difficult thing for anyone, especially your mother to hear.

Throughout this book-writing journey, my author and I spent many hours on video calls. We talked about my story, and I'd answer any questions she had. We followed that same pattern when interviewing my mom, so I have some insight that we learned from her journey through my troubles. Here are some of her feelings and memories, in her words and from her heart.

Life was really difficult for a while before Brennan was born. It was when I was pregnant with him that his father, Brian, really became abusive. He was never really abusive with the kids, he mostly took it out on me, but I was always worried. What if he didn't stop with me? What if I couldn't protect my children? I knew I just couldn't let that happen.

Brennan was my baby and the sweetest little boy a mom could ask for. Every night he would come into my room and give me a kiss goodnight! He was always happy, and as he grew up, he turned into the class clown. Some of this was a cover for the pain we later learned he was experiencing, but you would never have known what he was hiding when you looked at him.

He was always outside doing something. To this day, he can't stay still for very long. Whether it was playing some type of sport or some other activity, he was always on the go. He loved to camp and always looked forward to trips to the cabin. A true outdoorsman, he loved being out in nature. As I think back, knowing now what he was battling on the inside, I think being outside and in nature was a way for him to escape the pain, if only for a little while. Even today, he will hop on his motorcycle and travel to a lake or wilderness area to just be alone with his thoughts.

So, when Brennan was just a toddler, maybe a

little older than that, I decided we couldn't live there any longer. I did what any mom would do to protect her children. I left. I took a huge leap of faith and moved us into a group home—a sort of shelter—for a while. As you can imagine, that didn't go over well with my husband. The threats continued, and he became enraged. He left thirty to forty messages a day, and now he was threatening to kill my children. I knew I had done the right thing, but I was terrified.

As Brennan continued to grow up, he really poured himself into sports. He's a very competitive person (and simply hates to lose), so he committed himself to being the best possible. This was very evident later on when he joined the military. But It was also these sports that contributed to his downfall. As most young athletes sometimes face, Brennan got injured a lot. Ultimately these injuries sent him down a dark path. Injuries meant medicine to mask the pain. These medicines were highly addictive, and as a result, he became an addict at a very young age. I believe he was sixteen when I first realized he had a problem. However, he'd had a problem for much longer. He had just kept it really hidden. He was slowly showing signs that he was not the same little, loveable boy I'd known.

As his additions took hold and he turned into someone I no longer recognized, it tore me apart. I never stopped loving Brennan, and in fact, I think I love him more than I ever thought possible, seeing how he's overcome challenge after challenge. If I said it was easy to love during the dark times, I'd be lying. It was difficult. There were some very, very dark times, and I had to step up and choose the difficult road of tough love. I had to choose not to let him come back home for the 100'th time when he was homeless yet again. It was the hardest thing I've ever done, but I knew in my heart I had to do it to ultimately help him. I know it seems backward, and it was met with objection, but sometimes as a mom, you have to do what you feel is right. I'll be honest, though, and let you know that I did have my doubts, and I cried more tears for my son and what he was going through than I could even count, but I stand by my decisions. I never stopped loving. I never stopped praying.

Whatever you are going through, or whatever your children or loved ones are going through, here is my advice to you. It's okay to cry. It's okay to scream. It's okay to be frustrated and mad. But, whatever you do, NEVER—and I mean NEVER—stop praying for and loving them.

I don't know what you are going through, or maybe what the road ahead looks like, but for me, I continually pray for each one of my children each and every day. Whether they are having the best days or the worst days of their lives, they always know that this momma is on her knees praying to our Heavenly Father to watch over them and protect them.

Now, do you see why I love this woman so much! God knew exactly what I would need for the path my life was going to take.

I've talked about the horrible relationship, if you can even use that word relationship, with my biological father. But I want to also share with you some great memories and love I've experienced with my stepfather. He was the man by my mother's side when she was dealing with all of my issues and demons. It's difficult enough to grow into a family, but to walk that line of being the stepparent isn't easy.

Jeff came into my mother's life and our lives at a time when we all needed him the most, and for that, I will be eternally grateful. I'd also like to share some of my thoughts and memories growing up with him in my life.

Keep reading...

CHAPTER SEVEN

HOW A DAD'S LOVE FOR MOM AFFECTS THEIR KIDS

The way dads treat moms is super important for their kids who are constantly watching and learning about relationships from both parents.

How A Dad's Love For Mom Effects Their Kids

We have often seen children of broken homes having psychological and behavioral issues. Wait! What about children who have their parents together but not happy with each other?

Relationships at home matter a lot when it comes to kids. The relationship between both parents is top on this list. When a husband and wife become father and mother, their support for each other becomes more important. When parents show this support to each other, kids will naturally follow in their footsteps. But when kids see disrespect between their parents, they will also be disrespectful towards others when they grow up.

Children watch how dad treats their mother. They watch him giving her compliments or appreciating her efforts, or otherwise demotivating her or ignoring her.

If your relationship with your life partner is based on disrespect and anger, it will eventually appear in your kids also. Similarly, if you ignore each other or not acknowledge each other's efforts, then kids will also learn how not to express their feelings for themselves and for others. So, this chain of silence and no communication will continue on and on.

A gentleman or even a man, a human, doesn't scream or raise his hand on any woman. A gentleman doesn't abuse physically or verbally. If a dad does so, he is harming his kid's personalities and putting their future at risk. When kids see abusive relationships at home, they start hating relationships and so become abusive themselves when they grow up.

Express Your Love

A warm hug, a goodbye, or goodnight kiss to your wife is important in front of your children so that they know and feel the warmth of loving relationships and develop positivity about the concept of home and family. Physical touch is important to show to your kids. But don't mix up this kind of love with intimacy in the bedroom.

Show Gratitude

Show gratitude to your wife for being a great wife and great mom. Appreciate her efforts in front of your kids. This way they will develop more respect for their mother and also for their father i.e. you. Whether your wife is a housewife or works outside of the home, she needs your appreciation because it means a lot to her. And it also means a lot to your kids.

Give Your Support

Play your role as a father and be supportive of your wife in the upbringing of your children. After all, you are equally responsible for their upbringing. So, helping your wife with home chores or kids' stuff will make kids feel special and loved. If you and your life partner will fight over the division of responsibilities as father and mother, then chances are that your kid will feel like a burden, and it will eventually lead to negative things like depression, escape, or in some cases, suicidal attempts.

Give Space

Giving space to your spouse is also important to let your kids know that their father and mother have a life and identity as an individual because they need some time for themselves too. This way your kids will learn how to give space to others and not always nagging others.

Spend Quality Time Together

Spending quality time with each other is very important both for healthy relationships and healthy upbringing of kids. When kids see their father taking out time for their mother and spending quality time together, they grow well emotionally and feel positive about relationships. Play games together with your wife and kids, go for outings on weekends, and on a vacation at least once a year if you are able.

Use Right Language & Communicate Well

Language and communication is the key to any successful relationship. It will prove to your kids its importance if you do it. Talk to your wife politely, respectfully, and call her by sweet names like "Honey" or "Darling" in front of your kids. Tell your kids through your words and actions that their mother is respectable and special for them.

Hence, when the father and mother are there for each other and kids watch them being each other's support, they will develop a positive outlook and will not only become adults with positive thoughts and good emotional development, but they will also like the idea of marriage and relationships in future[7].

Keep reading...

7 Samira Khan, "Dad's Love For Mom Affects Their Kids," Moms, 2021, https://www.moms.com/how-dads-love-mom-affects-kids/.

CHAPTER EIGHT

SALVATION

Let's be real for a moment. Life can suck sometimes, but through faith, I get out of bed each morning and fight my battles with God in my heart and by my side.

Brennan R. Wegener

God's been keeping me alive for a very specific purpose, and I'm getting close to truly acknowledging His love for me. As I look back at my journey to accepting Jesus Christ as my personal Lord and Savior, there are three really specific events in my life that played a role.

Back when I was in Madison, I was preparing to take my own life (again). I had previously tried several times. One time, in particular, I tried to put a gun to my mouth, but it never fired when I pulled the trigger. The very next day, it fired without incident at the firing range. This happened more than once.

This time in Madison, I was in the hospital, I think I've

already mentioned this time, but it bears mentioning again. Remember, I was in the hospital, and there was a demon presence in my room. Somehow I had talked the nurses into leaving me to shower in private, and when they did, I locked the door so that I could hang myself in the shower. As I put my hand up to the shower nozzle, it was as if someone poured a hot jar of honey on my head, and it traveled down over my body. This was followed by a vision of God placing His hand on my head and hearing Him speak directly to me. That was the first event.

Event number two took place in early 2016. I was in the middle of intense, dark depression. I was homeless at the time and feeling very hopeless about my future. I went to church and, while there, I felt called to walk down the center aisle. When I did, I was immediately tormented by demons, and I physically collapsed on the floor. There were 4–5 people praying over me, exhausting themselves in prayer to deliver me from these demons. I was baptized five months later in August.

I continued to slip back into my old habits and drifted away from my new Savior. It was then that two pastors, Scott and Darnisha Taylor, prayed over me in the presence of my mom and my girlfriend at the time, Crystal. Through intense prayer at their house and then followed by more intercessors at church, I finally felt the demons leaving every organ of my body.

If I said that life has been all sunshine and rainbows since I finally was rid of those demons, I'd be lying. My road has been anything if not the toughest journey I've ever faced. Each day is a struggle, and I've digressed more than a few times since that day. But I can tell you that I try to make each day a little better than the day before. I pray daily and sometimes minute by minute just to get through each day.

I believe in deliverance. I also know that God has given me the gift of recognizing the supernatural. I see visions and receive messages about others that are always correct.

I want to tell you that even though my journey has been anything but linear, I love God with all of my heart and soul and will stop at nothing to spread the good news of salvation to the ends of the earth. No demon. No addiction. No past abuse. Nothing can stop me.

I will be honest with you; I'm not sure why God allowed my abuse and addictions to grip me as hard as they did. But I do know that God saw me through the darkest of days. He kept me safe and brought me through to the other side of darkness to see the light of His glory. The least I can do is tell my story so that others can see what a great God He really is.

What are you dealing with today? What demons have a hold on you? What are you battling? Maybe it's not you, but someone special to you. It doesn't matter what it is. Really, it doesn't. God loves you just the same.

Maybe you've seen or heard this analogy before. Say you have a $100 bill. Take that $100 bill and wad it up in a ball.

Open it back up and show its wrinkles and folds. It's still a $100 bill. It didn't lose its value. Now take that same $100 bill and soak it in a mud puddle or rub it around in the dirt. Pick it back up. It's still a $100 bill. Take it through the wash, step on it, or whatever you choose. It's still a $100 bill. It has lost ***none*** of its value. ***you*** are that $100 bill. Nothing you've done or been through can make you lose your value to God our Father. Nothing.

Keep reading...

CHAPTER NINE
LOVE FINDS ME

The year was 2018. I'd found the Lord. I was staying clean and sober. It had still been a rough year, though, but it was about to turn around in the most unexpected and beautiful ways. Her name was Nikki.

I found my ***match***. Apparently, I was the ***man*** of God she was looking for, and our attraction and connection appeared to be perfect from the first meeting. I remember spending the day together down by a river, sitting on a rock. We were just talking. We were talking about our views—on life, marriage, faith, and even politics. Could it really be that God had brought me my soul mate? I was cautious but very excited!

In the meantime, God decided to throw a little wrench in our new love story.

We met in June and went on our first date in July. During that time, God had placed it on my heart that I needed to head home by myself to be a present father with my kids. During all this time, Nikki and I had already been on four or five dates, so things were definitely heading in the right direction. But how was I to ever make this decision to go home and leave the woman that God had brought me? So, I decided to be open with her and not only tell her about what I felt God was leading me to but also about my past. All of it. I held nothing back. I wanted her to know it all. I had always been looking for someone who was also looking for more than a few dates. I wanted, I longed, I prayed for someone who would want a relationship, but up until this point, I'd always been meeting the wrong people.

The First Impressions

Nikki thought I was a catch from the first moment she laid eyes on me. I mean, how can you blame her? Okay, I told you from the start I'd be transparent, so no, it didn't quite go down like that. She did, however, appreciate that it looked like I made an effort. Apparently, she thought I was clean and well dressed. Hey, I'll take that!

For me, on the other hand, I thought she wasn't going to show based on my track record. So, when she did, I knew there was something special about her already. And by the second time we met, I knew she was the one I wanted to be with. She was super chill and a very cool girl. I could tell she was special.

After only about two weeks, I told her I loved her because I could just tell we had moments of undeniable chemistry. She, on the other hand, never said it back to me. Come on... she left me hanging! All kidding aside, I knew she was the one I wanted to be with, so when she said she wanted to pray through it, I gave her all the space she needed.

Truly giving her the space she needed, what else could I do but tell her I loved her all day, every day. So one night, as we were enjoying a bottle of wine, I wrote "I love you" on the wine bottle and passed it to her. Much to my surprise, she turned to me and said, "I love you too." I nearly fell over!

I continued to share my past with her. I wanted her to know everything. There could be no part of my past that was skipped over or even watered down. For her to really love me, I knew she had to know all of me. And she did.

She continued to pray for us and for direction. She was asking God for signs all the time, and He would answer her through answers I'd give her when she'd asked me something. She would ask God for a sign, but when I would respond a certain way, it would be a complete affirmation that only God could have confirmed with her. I had no knowledge of any of it but was used by God to answer Nikki. She would question things in my past or question things that I was saying and go to God in prayer. It's pretty cool that God used me as His vessel to answer her.

I was in the middle of a pretty big pull from God during this time, too, where He was putting in me the urge to go back to Wisconsin to work on myself and be with my boys for a bit. I'd always been thinking that I needed to head back home to take time for myself—time I'd really never had with all my relapses, treatment centers, homelessness, and constant moving.

Nikki was fine with me moving, and we decided to make this thing work long distance. And we did! We never went more than three weeks without being together. We met in June. We went on our first date in July. I moved near the end of July, and the months apart only made us stronger. We married in December. This was a great ending to 2018 and an even better beginning to 2019.

In 2019, just as Nikki and I were adjusting to our new life as a married couple, I was struggling with depression and PTSD. Nikki was supportive, but I could tell this was something she wasn't accustomed to handling. She was a trooper, though.

Then Came 2020

Where do I begin? The world would soon be overcome by a little virus that no one had ever heard of—virus that would literally shut down the entire planet. The senseless murder of an unarmed black man would set in motion riots against police brutality from every corner of the United States, and race relations would become a polarizing agenda for what seemed like every American. Add to it that it was an election year, and the political divide had never been greater.

2020 was just the perfect storm with sickness, death, anger, unrest, and violence in cities and homes across America. I don't know many people who were not touched in some way by the events of 2020.

I will not put all our dirty laundry out for the world to see, but I will tell you that our marriage and our love were not strong enough to withstand all of these outside stressors. As of the printing of this book, we are in the process of finalizing our divorce.

The love I thought I'd found was no more.

Keep reading...

CHAPTER TEN

MIDNIGHT ARRIVES

In October 2018, I adopted the love of my life. Okay, well, not entirely in the sense you may be thinking. I'm sure you've seen people all around you that have a service or emotional support animal by their side. While there is usually some debate on the validity of an emotional support animal, a service animal is much different. A service animal is generally paired with an owner who has specific needs the animal, a dog, in this case, fulfills. Tasks that these service animals perform are directly related to a person's needs. As an example, a guide dog helps someone who is blind or visually impaired navigate their environment.

I reached out to a well-known and well-respected organization that provides service dogs and started the process of qualifying for a service dog. Once I made the request, Midnight and I were matched together. But it was a little more involved than just sending me home with him. We went through an intensive six-month training period to learn about each other. It was love at first sight, and I don't know what I ever did without him.

When I'm experiencing anxiety, having trouble with my PTSD, or in the midst of a panic attack, Midnight is there to help me. He'll even lay his weight on me during the night when I'm having one of my many night terrors. When we're out in public, Midnight is always watching my "six" and crosses in front of me when people are walking towards me or appear to be coming at me. When I'm shaking, he'll either put his big paw on my foot to comfort me or if I'm sitting, he'll rest his head on my knee.

During the writing of this book, Christina and I would regularly communicate through video conference calls and try to introduce our two boxers to each other. She has a white boxer named Bella. While I thought it was cute to get them to try and look at each other on the computer screen, they never quite took a liking to each other. Mostly they were just confused, wondering what we were asking them to do. That's boxers for you.

Now that I'm out in the community speaking at Veteran's events or meeting with organizations, Midnight has become something of a celebrity. I mean, who can resist him. He's quite the good-looking fella. Be sure to look out for future books where Midnight "tells" his side of the story and how he has a big job to do taking care of me.

Keep reading...

CHAPTER ELEVEN
HEALING FORWARD

While this book was in the process of being finished up, I was having an especially difficult day. I may have bitten off more than I could chew, and I was feeling very overwhelmed. So, what's a guy to do? I wrote a post on Facebook just to vent a little, but mostly write a heartfelt post to my mom. My post is below, and her unscripted response follows. Both are unedited and copied straight from their online posts. I think this sums our love up beautifully.

To My Mom

As most of you all know, I'm an open book and very vocal about mental health and issues that come with PTSD and TBI's and my childhood. After four straight, insane months of launching a ministry and twelve years of speaking engagements, even through my struggles and five years of writing a book and other events, and help from a few friends, I pretty much have been a lone wolf one-man team. I've been running nonstop, helping others and holding and speaking at events and meetings, and doing anything and everything (to the best of my ability) to be there for and help others. For some reason, yesterday, I was so physically and mentally exhausted from this past week that I had one of the lowest nights and thoughts about myself in quite some time. Feelings of guilt, shame, feeling worthless and like what I'm doing isn't even helping people and obviously having some spiritual warfare and feelings of emptiness drawing me down, and the walls caving in and having panic as if I couldn't breathe and was dying.

My mom helped as always by talking to me about what I'm doing and how many people I've helped and reminded me that I'm right where I need to be and just need to keep recharging and believe in myself and remember not to listen to the bad thoughts of myself that come flowing in like raging waters and today I feel recharged again. God recharges me every single day. Thank you, Mom, for everything. Every day is Mother's Day appreciation to me.

So. here are some words for you today...

Mom, growing up I know I didn't always tell you how much I care about you. Now that I'm older, I can see how much you sacrificed for me, and I want to say that I'm so grateful for all you did. You have been so selfless and giving. Thank you from the bottom of my heart.

Because of you, I have the vision to reach for my dreams and the grit to push through the challeng-

es that are in my way. Thank you for making me strong. You are the best mom a guy could ever have!

Mom, you're my lifeline, my shoulder to cry on, my mentor. Thank you for always being there for me to talk to and letting me know that things will be okay.

Mom, I could never even hope to express just how much appreciation I hold in my heart for you, my loving mom. You have helped me in the toughest of times and you have celebrated by my side in the best of times. I am forever thankful for and to you. I love you with everything I have and more.

Thank you for being my mom[8].

Thank you for being my Rock!

To my son. (My mom's response.)

Thanks so much for your beautiful post and words. Means a lot to me. But honestly, it's pretty simple... a mother's love for her children is unconditional! No matter how many mistakes, we love our children through it, guide them, love them, support them, reprimand them, and hope they grow and learn from it all. We ALL slip up and make mistakes and we ALL have our crap, but we support and push each other through it with no judgment. Our family has been through our share of pain, trauma, heartbreak, and loss, but we persevere and push through,

8 "101 Heartfelt Thank You Mom Messages and Quotes," Future of Working, 2021, https://futureofworking.com/thank-you-mom-messages-and-quotes/.

but most importantly, with and through our faith and trust in our God. Proud of all you are doing, but with that said, there IS a time for rest, and I know how hard it is for you to slow down... but some days, you just need to BE STILL and be with God, and yes, then He will always recharge us. 🩶🩶

CHAPTER TWELVE
HEALING FORWARD

Rejoice always, pray without ceasing, give thanks in all circumstances; for this is the will of God in Christ Jesus for you.

1 Thessalonians 5:16–18 (ESV)

What better way to move forward in healing and faith than by helping others overcome challenges in their lives and find hope in Jesus Christ.

In May of 2021, I launched my charity, ***A Journey to the Light,*** to do just that. I want to spread the love and hope of Jesus to all who are hurting. With the help of my service dog, Midnight, I am hoping to do my part.

What started as simply a way to give back to the veterans who have given and sacrificed so much for our country has just exploded into a full ministry. In its simplest and truest form, through *A Journey to the Light,* I advocate for first responders, support our veterans, advocate and assist those with addictions,

PTSD, and those experiencing trauma, plus offer crisis response to those in need.

Back in 2017, I completed training through the Sacramento (CA) County Sheriff's Department to become a certified Chaplain, and as a result, I am now (as of the publishing of this book) the State Appointed Chaplain for the Military Motorcycle Association and the State Chaplain for Post 243 of the American Legion. I also partner with local and regional organizations such as area churches, those fighting the sex trafficking industry, and various nonprofit agencies.

I work hard to support our veterans, and I am currently working on legislation and grants to find funding through the Veteran's Affairs office. I'm looking to fill in the needs gap that our veterans face when looking for assistance. If I can help ease the burden even a little, it's more than worth the work involved.

Additionally, I've begun a partnership with an organization that provides support dogs for people of all walks of life and needs. There are so many people struggling in assisted living facilities that could use the support of a dog. This program helps make those connections possible.

As if this was not enough, there's something else I'm very excited about that happens to be a first of its kind. I'm partnering with local employers to be able to recruit to fill open positions. Of course, my focus is recruiting and helping veterans find great jobs, but I also get to act as their advocate within their new employer. What this means is that if once they begin working and they experience some challenges relating to their mental health, I work with their employer to get them the time off that they need. This time off is then paid, so they are not affected financially. So many times veterans and those with addictions, trauma, and other challenges don't have advocates in the workplace. They feel alone. They may also fall victim to workplace prejudices. With this program, they have me. I'm their advocate. I help with their management to get them the time off and, if needed, the help to thrive in their new role.

As you've followed my journey through these pages, undoubtedly, you may have thought about similarities in your own life or in the life of someone you care about. Please know that you don't have to go this road alone. I would be honored to talk to you and even try to get you connected with someone who can help if I'm unable to.

Feel free to reach out to me through my website: www.brennanwegener.com. Whether you need prayer, someone to talk to, or even information about *A Journey to the Light,* don't be a stranger. If there is one thing that I want you to take away from these pages and my story, it's that I'm here for you. You are not alone. There is a way out of the darkness, and His name is Jesus Christ. My journey isn't over, and neither is yours.

I love you,
Brennan

JESUS IS
LORD

THE WARRIOR

CALIFORNIA

CHAPLAIN
SHEPARD

ABOUT THE AUTHOR

Brennan Wegener

Brennan is a father of two boys and a disabled Iraq and Afghanistan veteran who has struggled with addiction and alcoholism until he found Christ and his faith. He loves helping and guiding those who are lost and struggling to find their faith and guide them to improve their circumstances. As a retired Airforce Security Forces veteran and prior law enforcement officer, his passion is giving back to veterans, law enforcement, and first responders. Brennan has proven this by serving as a Sheriff's chaplain for his local county sheriff's department, the lead chaplain for his community Legion Post, a commander and the chaplain for the military veterans motorcycle association for the state of WI. Brennan is a proud owner of a veteran store and an advocate for people who are struggling with mental health.

We need to break the stigma with mental health, PTSD, suicide, and have better resources and support available to accomplish this mission. My goal is to save every person I can with God's guidance.

Brennan enjoys taking trips with his children and service pup midnight, working out, riding his Harleys, hiking, doing live podcasts, and also speaking to the church, audiences, and concerts to share his testimony and will be accepting book signing engagements, tours, and will travel to speaking invitations.

You can reach out to Brennan at

Brennanwegener.com

Ajourneytothelight27@gmail.com

920-266-3910

Christina L. Sussmann

Christina is an award-winning screenwriter and sought-after ghostwriter, having written more than a dozen features and just as many children's books. She got her start writing thanks to an afternoon conversation with her (*then*) music minister who had her writing the drama, dialog, and stage directions for the church Christmas ministry production (*that just so happened to have at least a half dozen ticketed performances scheduled*). Once she saw her vision come to life and the audience reacting where she hoped they would, she was hooked. The rest, as they say, is history.

She is the over-the-moon-proud mom of her twenty-five-year-old son, Tyler, and just-as-proud-mom of her rescue boxer named Bella. She loves to travel and regularly visits her son in Florida. She is a member of Greenford Christian Church in Greenford, Ohio, and can usually be found singing as a member of their praise team a couple of times a month.

During the writing of this book, Christina's love, Mark, passed away after a very short and sudden battle with Covid. You can find a memory Christina shared about Mark in an early chapter.

Cancer took the life of her mother when Christina was just a new mom herself. One thing she overheard her mother say to a group of friends about her serves as motivation to this day. She said... (Christina) **"can't tell a joke to save her life, but she can tell an amazing story."**

Christina would like to dedicate this book to her family—Tyler (her son), Howard (her father), Carl (her brother), Liz (her sister-in-law), and Annie (her favorite niece). Thank you for all of your support and encouragement. Thank you also to Brennan for believing in me. Look out, world!

Words of advice: Always pray about it. Take pictures; you'll be glad you did later. And when given a choice, always pick the first or the last row of the roller coaster... the line may be shorter, but the middle is just too boring! Don't forget to buckle up, reach for the sky and enjoy the ride.

Christina can be reached at:

susschristina@gmail.com or 330.429.4803

www.christinasussmann.com

www.theaffordableghostwriter.com

www.christinalouiseagency.com

You can't expect God to bless what you won't hand over to him.

REFERENCES

"101 Heartfelt Thank You Mom Messages and Quotes." 2021. Future of Working. 2021. https://futureofworking.com/thank-you-mom-messages-and-quotes/.

"AFNOA - Air Force Song (Old and New) by Major Robert Crawford, 1939." n.d. American Airforce Navigator Observer Association [AFNOA]. Accessed November 5, 2021. https://www.afnoa.org/afsong.html.

Ellis, Sam. 2020. "What Do Feathers Symbolize In The Bible?" Catholics & Bible. 2020. https://catholicsbible.com/what-do-feathers-symbolize-in-the-bible/.

Fiset, Jocelyn. 2021. "9/11 by the Numbers: Victims, Hijackers, Aftermath, and More Facts about September 11, 2001." ABC7 San Francisco. 2021. https://abc7news.com/911-september-11-victims-facts-about-how-many-planes-were-hijacked-on/11006480/.

Khan, Samira. 2021. "Dad's Love For Mom Affects Their Kids." Moms. 2021. https://www.moms.com/how-dads-love-mom-affects-kids/.

"On 9/11, 102 Minutes That Changed America." 2016. Insider. 2016. https://www.businessinsider.com/afp-on-911-102-minutes-that-changed-america-2016-9.

"Shalom Headlines." 2020. Posts | Facebook. 2020. https://www.facebook.com/shalomheadlines/posts/demonic-world-and-how-its-work-the-term-demon-is-derived-from-the-greek-word-dai/121101616298139/.

CPSIA information can be obtained
at www.ICGtesting.com
Printed in the USA
FSHW011627010222

9 781685 562243